T0365355

ISBN: Softcover   978-1-5434-9541-6
        EBook   978-1-5434-9540-9

Print information available on the last page

Rev. date: 04/16/2019

To order additional copies of this book, contact:
Xlibris
0800-443-678
www.xlibris.co.nz
Orders@ Xlibris.co.nz

Life
Most Complex Problems

The Real Reason for Our Being

Betsyboo

with the gods on the outside of our lives
this way they help us on the inside our family trees , and on levels

THE UNIVERSAL TRAVELLERS.

The unexplained wisdom words family trees
ON LEVELS TOP MIDDLE BOTTOM
BRANCHES OUT WAITING TO BE UNDERSTOOD
DOWN THE FAMILY TREES

THE UNRAVELING OFTHE UNIVERSE,
IN OUR WISDOM WORDS WAY

PREFACE

THE BEGINNING, THE END
THE FIRST, THE LAST
FROM A-Z, FROM 1-9
MY LIFE
IN LIFE MOST COMPLEX PROBLEMS
HOW PRECIEVE WITH THEORIES RESEARCH.
ON REASON 4 OUR BEING
THROUGH VISION WISE WORDS
VERSES FROM THE BIBLE.
LEARN SOME THING KNEW EVER DAY GROW
IN BODY SOLE HELP UNRAVEL LIFE
BIG JIG SAW PUZZLES OF HUMAN SURVIVAL

THE LAND, THE SEAS, THE AIR, SKY, CLOUDS.
ALL MAKE UP OUR LIFE'S SPAN PATTERNS

branches out onto level understanding
like branches of the tree

PREFACE

I'm a widow, raised 4 children alone and was a rape victim, age 15, as a child always ask question why this and why that about material possessions an life, but never really ever got a satisfaction reply as to believe I don't think our parents really knew the full answer, and so they put old-time sayings in words there, I suppose they mean to get back to a child with the right answer. one day. The main key to life and progress in time is to honour thy father and mother learn from there mistakes, correct them in your children then they in there's whats not understood in words goes back up to parent to work out the wisdom of them, this way prevents history from repeating its self in ever second generations,

To start with, how it came about that I realize there had to be more to our lives then what we were living, growing up married children then dies god must create us for another reason than just that. so I set about thinking about my childhood wonders and vision id saw. To look at things in a clear light day and by seeing the full picture of life, I saw images from that all we do on earth and created in the sky's energy force, universe.

If I go back to my childhood around 4-5 year old and remember things that formed my life and belief in gods, I remember a family incidence, once that was as real I always wonder why and what the meaning behind it was, as did one something wrong and got growled at for taking candle in under a bed, I was put outside in the dark, as I sat there crying I heard a voice, say to me, why are you crying, I said I was afraid of the dark, the voice said to me don't cry, don't be afraid of the dark.

These words never left me over years always wonder who it was that said it to me. who was the spiritual voice I heard, over the year I had several answers to my wondering, at age of 40plus the true answer came to me, what this voice meant as by not being afraid of the darkness, it was part the universe in time that different cultures lived, each culture has a sound barrier between each other, and the reason why some people born of different coloured skin, I waited for the right answer from god at age 40 rights message came from God to me now I do know the true answer of why we born in different parts time, and gap between each culture.

THE TEAR DROPS PICTURE

THE TENSION HOLDS CLOUDS TOGETHER CHANGES SHAPES SIZES

THE THINNED OUT CLOUDS SKY AND ENERGY FORCE

ABOUT THIS BOOK

But as my life went on, once again I heard, a voice that said to me for what reason should I let you into heaven, as I travelled in times, I had to think, as there would be no satisfaction, being in heaven by myself, So my reply to this voice in thoughts only was I didn't want to go to heaven unless everybody else came with me, so if that was one god's voices he sent me back to help others understand. what he intended to send me, messages from the heavens to explain the visions he shows me.in the futures, this information on our passage in time did not come to me all at once, it came in through a period of years of putting together my own life words action deeds, but first I had to correct my past mistakes in others then go back to what I first remembered and start again, I've explained best in this book how to advance.

My thoughts were from time to time in short- like Jesus Gods funny and I booked it all up to Jesus hoped to Christ he paid, little did i know full impact that would happen with these word, he the gods lords almighty paying big time in wisdom words, our words and how they can be used to balance out weather patterns we start at being born, the we talk, we run, we walk, we fall down, we pick our selves up, life life that on levels we go to far, stop look and listen same words used crossing a road, three, meanings to every thing, spiritual one and a verbal one and a material possession one . Patience is a key in ever thing we think say do, our values we taught play big role in how we conduct our selves around others, my theories based on

Vision, research, thoughts, wonders action in my time of growing up, when I realized that there had to be more to our lives then getting old dying, I set out to find the reason 4 our being, being created just to die didn't seem to make since to me, so it taken years of trail error to understand this far, I didn't realize just how far my wonder would lead me with gods help and wisest ones, were ever one may be let wise words go free when they come back improve learn understand them

NO RHYME NOR REASON

No Rhymes Nor Reasons Pride or Prejudice or Blame.

UNSPOKEN WORDS We Reap What We Sow, Reading of the universe, wise words. And old time saying, songs nursery rhymes. Traveling on the Back of other Persons, PIGGYBACKS,LEAPFROG, from VISA VERSA, Turn back rotate wisdom words . White or yellow sun back to back, our action in material possessions life.

Time to understand the true meaning of partnerships and relationship and part they play in to the futures of next generations safety of this planets, and all human life, IN 1997 when the big comet went past earth. what i saw by vision was so unbelieveable. ,past present and ahead to further how it can be done. in fairness to all mankind. people have been having vision for year into past and ahead futures.

But so much, my mind couldn't comprehend what it all meant, with little research on universe, and over last 20 odd years IVe written down my visions and the answer came flowing. but not all at once it was overtimes,on the back of others. This Is a whole another story in its self . The bible was my next step to understand further and keep my belief in gods whom created us, the words in bible do represent the verses of our words. In the beginning, the end, the first, the last, from, AZ 1-9this we had to apply in our lives for next levels, to improve on, for one to sacrifice ones life upon god altar, we only getting it half right. open any door no one can shut, in our time.

Ever thing we think say do from day we born clings to our waist like a belt (or come back at us sometime in our life span)so the bible states go back to what you first knew and come to me again, first in life, is education learning read write reactions and thoughts but when born we are old. we stopped understanding further in wisdom words way. or improve further.

SMOKE SIGNALS IN CLOUD FORMATIONS

A PUFF OF SMOKE

ACTION WORDS IMAGES ALL MAKE UP THE CLOUD FORMATION

LIFE MOST COMPLEX PROBLEM
REASON 4 OUR BEING

MY INSPIRATIONAL WISDOM WORDS
IN TIME
FROM BIRTH TO ADULTHOOD
teach respect values dont touch whats not ones before their time
From adult hood to the bible
TRAVELLERS IN TIME.

understood wise wisdom words the family tree on levels

the family trees wise words of wisdom help each other to branch out then back to the trunk the main

What we do in between times is what carrry us through our life span, we reap what we sow, we can change coarse of actions any time we please to follow the wisdom words path. and listen to the messages sent from above, go back to what one first thought knew and then come back to me (the gods.)

We have stages = born= small letters. learn not l;earnt in life we grow and lean from. BORN first movement that clings to our waist like a belt, blink, stretch. cry out, from then on the pattern of our lives begin. We learnt to talk, walk and we fall down we get up again, this action repeated regularly, until one gets it right, same as our lives in gods wisdom words passage in time we take a step forward, in wisdom words then if not meant for one stop or step back wait for next level to catch up or go in another direction where movement is easy. when we reach 50plus time our lives is when the change in life happens, this to has two meaning change in life in body for women and a change in mind body and sole, the latter is. our past comes back at us, ever thing we thought said and done since born come in, as we reap what we sow, the good part is what mistake we did back in our childhood its all wisdom words and has a place in time, to be used, to balance weather out, We make these mistake against other as its a learning cue. But now in this day age we got to correct our mistakes against others so we can open up the passage thats blocking our way ahead, by correcting our mistakes, against others our body heals, as a cat has nine lives so does humans.

Each mistake we correct against another we get part of our full life back, nine lives 1-9 Best way in life is don't bite the hand that feeds one, people give support by just know when one need to be strong don't give money advise or blame, they are guided by gods to help anothers but they can't get through to dishonesty when person honest with them selve on all level the doorway to help another is open.

We found a way to stay alive in human form to eternity on earth and how it can be done in fairness to all mankind,man have been looking for the answer to this for centuries but never could find the way God intended us to follow, we got so far and stopped learning put material possession first ahead of life, and survival.

We all inclined to live to die instead of living to stay alive in human form, living for today and to hell with tomorrow only leads to early grave, gods created us to stay alive in human form until eternity on earth, the more we rotate our words understand wisdom of them the more we balance the weather and keep the elements from the universe at bay.

POEM 1903

HER JOY WAS DUTY HER LOVE WAS LAW, FOR ALL SAD WORDS OF TONGUE OR PEN THE SADDEST OF ALL ARE THESE

"AH WELL FOR US ALL SOME SWEET HOPE, LIES DEEPLY BURIED FROM HUMANS EYES AND IN THE HERE AFTER, ANGELS MAY ROLL THE STONE FROM ITS GRAVE AWAY .

HER JOY WAS DUTY, HER LOVE WAS LAW IT MIGHT HAVE BEEN

BLUE SKY CLEAR WATERY ENERGY FORCE

STORM CLOUD RISING FROM MIXED UP WISDOM WORDS

MIXTURE DIFFERENT ENERGY FORCES CREATES
CLOUDS FORM WEATHER PATTERNS

CINDERRELLA AND GOLDEN SLIPPERS,

A rolling stone gather no moss, tower of the four winds, turtle and the hare, old mother hubbard, mother goose, I'm a little tea pot, wise old owl, walk a crooked mile.

Adult meanings our action in our lives against others, we have learnt from, just nine of my favourites, like ten commandments, the ones we remember are the one we most likely to act, in our life span, against other, based one theories, vision, thoughts wonders, actions, from birth to adult hood. The action they forgot was we had to live by these rules, not say them, and blaming other when our own mistakes surfaced. Back in times of yesteryear.

Cinderella and golden slippers, this is one nursery ryhme that over centuries we all went out and copied. The actions how it originated was if one person wanted something or needed it the jealously of other would over shadow there thoughts and want same thing. right down all generation to thus far, we have copied the same action against others. JEALOUSLY = (wanting to be first, beter then another,) there is no I want or I said that in gods voculabury, spiritually or verbally when one a child one carry on like that. Cinderella, morals behind this nursery rhymes is as humans we all trieds to do is fit up same family tree path, when by branching out we could expaned and make more room for generation to come and spred out the energy force. As the path to this was easiest way, but we ended up with a tip at the top, with no where to go but down on our past mistakes.

JEALOUSLY = 131-14-5 (131) one can match these number up to any verse in bible and the verse match up to the words One The scroll the bible talks about has exactly what I'm trying to explain in words written on it, tells us how it can be done, words from jealously = SLY, SEA. YES, YELL, USE, the gods angry He the Devils and god took the first bet in time-- the reason being If Gods created humans they end up destroying each other, which over centuries has occurred. but at this time in our lives, we got way ahead devils work. I WAS ABOUT TO WRITE IT DOWN WHEN A VOICE. from heaven said "don't do that: their words are not to be revealed. These words that weren't to be spoken, are the swear words, that gods used when they got impatient with humans, this he used to handle the thunder, storm heat, and keep his pillars in place. There always be a reason being behind Gods ways and action, down to people Then the seventh angel blows his trumpet revealed the plan mysterious, through the ages ever since it was announced, the swear words we use today, but once broken down into numerology and verse its all wisdom words and has a place in time when it be used to help balance the weather patterns out one swear words We found... A way to stay alive in human form to eternity. on earth and how it can be done in fairness to all mankind, man has been looking for the answer to this for centuries but never could find the way God intended us to follow, we got so far. and stopped learning put material possession first ahead of life, and survival, we grew up hearing that God will have peace on earth as in heaven, it will be done, but he made us in his image to help him with his plan, was to stay alive in human form. the whole universe to conquer REMEMBER, NEXT TO JOIN UP VERSE FROM BIBLE We all heard at some time in our life, the words. GOD has his big book out in-universe, and he puts all our good and bad in it, wait till we ready to help us understand our mistakes, over time. and what part in time we need it to be used to, balance weather once we understand the wise words of our mistakes. and what part in time it be needed. our past mistakes are our correction into the future.

They also have said, it's written in the stars, falling star wisdom from our forefather and mothers.

gods made the seas the land and ever thing in on earth

the rock and the hard place, against a brick wall, our words
mistakes and unspoken words create the rock in front of us

once our past mistakes are corrected against others

then we lift the rock and open the door thus far no one can shut

TURTLE AND THE HARE

The hare raced ahead of the turtle for his own selfish agenda. The turtle took his time and got the path way through to perfection. Our old time saying came from this action,was cleaning their bodies not their minds, (they left there mistakes on other or against other which block other view to see what's in front of them, they were aren't just nursery rhymes, of words they are our future passage in time. and the old time saying not just words, they part of a full sentence our parents couldn't put together to explain what their subconscious minds know, when the hare raced ahead of the turtle he thought he knew ever thing, but when he finished to take the glory he found he left all his mistakes in word and deeds behind on another. this other understood the wisdom of the words so his level was made easy and the one whom raced ahead, had to go back to square one and start again or take a step back, wait(learn patience)with action and mouth

The wise old owl sat in a tree(family tree) the less he spoke the more he heard, means, more he watched the more he learnt from other mistakes against others, by keep an open mind with out blame or prejuiced, words old time saying, silence is golden, never speak until spoken to, ask verbally what one dose not understand.

Walk a crooked mile. One only needs to say one word out line and it will mutiply around others ten fold. (These nursery rhymes originated for children to keep their little minds down on levels. They can understand about life, until old enough to understand the adults meaning to them)

(WE BRING STUFF TO OUR MIND DON'T AND CAN'T UNDERSTAND AS WISDOM OF THE WORDS COULD POSSIBLE BELONG TO ANOTHER FAMILY TREE)

We all have a different personality to handle life, in life we bring ever one up to same level as another in there thinking and actions we get the repeating our selves and history (will) repeat its self ever second generations.

We can prevent this by correcting past mistake in children them in theirs and then back to parents to understand wisdom words what comes in on one.

So when we get to the change of life if we back track in to our own past we have lived then we find it easier to correct what we left behind on others

the clear fresh energy force
mix with rest clouds dilutes the tension anger smooth the way for
stars moon to shine the wisdom of the energy force in the sky

FROM BIRTH TO BIBLE

We all gets part bible come in on us sometime in our lives part being lived and part being seen by vision and part that are theories, of others minds of wonder. wonder the next step to wisdom. Most verse in bibles are parts where our forefather and mother have already corrected their generations mistakes. The answer are in the bible, when one know where and how to look, As our minds all want to understand different part in time of our wonder, over years different part bible verse represent this.

To help ones understand a way how it can be done, and I might add we must keep the bible in our lives memories, and generations as if the worst ever did happen we will always find our way back in time. like I believe has happened before. We made a mistake broke universe apart and now this time in history we had to start again from scratch, history shows hidden buried cities from centries back so the elements from the universe could suffucated earth, less population then . Jesus said go out mulitply as the plan for future survival gods knew we needed more population to balance out clouds formations, and us as human would play biggest role ever, in help all to stay alive in human form.

Parts bible what we learn and understand thus far as we being taught apart from values respect from home we had to live by these values to get the full picture, of our lives what comes back at us in our lives is the miss understand of a sentence or answer that we asked about, as no one can put the full sentence together of our wisdom words past present . together as between the answer and question is other family trees word wisdom and it prevents us from connecting up the whole sentence we want to say, this in turn caorses us to branch out in family trees, connect together with other like minded ones but when its all over we have to go back to our parents to understand further, as if we leave our parents behind then it won't solve any ones problems, old time saying. Never put young person head on older persons shoulders. If we live by this then we won't go far wrong in time.

THE SHORT CUT TO BITS AND PIECES BOOK OF ALL LIFE SPAN. AS INDIVIDUALS. Bits and pieces TO A LONG LIFE OF LIFE MOST COMPLEX PROBLEM, REAL REASON 4 OUR BEING.

This book is an open book as it represents the words past around for centries down generations as to the bibles different meanings actions and thoughts all applied to the history of life, based on theories, vision, oldtime saying, songs and nursery rhymes, s it open to any and all whom have thoeries of what they determine life about, based on self taught, values, patience unspoken words, and the sileince of yearteryear. Our primitive way of life is still very active. in families, AND HOW WE APPROACH OTHER OR AGAINST OTHERS, We CAN't GET THROUGH ANY WHERE UNTIL WE corrected past mistake in our children, them in theirs then back to parents.

KEEP OPEN MIND READ ON

HOW IT CAN BE DONE IN FAIRNESS TO ALL MANKIND,

ON LEVELS UNDERSTAND OUR WISDOM OF OUR WORDS,

AND AS WE GO WE BALANCE OUT THE WEATHER PATTERNS.

TO CREATE A PASSAGE THROUGH TIME FOR ALL HUMAN

SURVIVAL. AND SAFETY OF THIS PLANET.

BASED ON NURSERY RHYMES, OLD TIME SONGS, OLD TIME SAYING, OUR WORDS ACTIONS THOUGHTS AND VISIONS. AND WE COULD FIND THE ANSWER IN VERSES IN THE BIBLE.

As I was told one day that world oyster and all one need to do was pluck it, this is so true in life, but what would your mind decide it meant. The material possession path or gods wisdom words passage, to my mind at the time was the material possession I thought this chap meant but know what I know now its the whole damn shooting box thats out their waiting for us to pluck out, our family wisdom words understand them and improve on them. Our words of jest over our traveller journey in our life span, these words do in deed have two meaning one spiritual one the other material possessions one.

Based on theories, wonder vision, nursery rhymes, old time songs, old time saying that being said in family and family trees, lot families had saying and wise words, leveled them out, as they knew they had to be improved further down the generations to understand, but in this day age as some learnt further ahead then others the levels need to be of man women so to explain to others, some relate to a man and another relate to women, visa versa. EVER THEORIES IS IMPORTANT AS IT WILL BE USED IN A PART IN TIME, TO HELP BALANCE THE WEATHERS.

DONT WORRY IN YOUR THEORIES YOU FIND YOU MIGHT REPEAT YOUR SELF, As the sentence come back at one, (like it does when one mistake surface) then its more wise wisdom words being added or improved on. We reap what we sow, in all walks life, and this is good thing as we have the chance to improve furthers in wisdom words tell the whole story

LIFE MOST COMPLEX PROBLEMS

JUST a tip the ice berg how it can be done our words our thoughts go a long way in balancing out the weather patterns, UNSPOKEN WORDS, THE TIME TO HAVE THEM PUT INTO written words now the time to have them spoken and written down, so all can understand and improve further in time.

THE REAL REASON 4 OUR BEING

THERE MORE TO OUR LIVES THEN MEETS THE EYES, ON LEVELS

ALL actions written or spoken, we start with our birth, movrment, talk, crawl, stand up fall down, life like that we take step forward, OF UNDERSTANDING, One step at a time, foreward. and don't touch whats no your, before ones time. Take a step back wait, (patience), FORWARD THINKERS. patience is a verture. . forward thinkimg is when one steps forward with out touching another life verbally or spiritually basically women known as the foreward thinkers, but some where some lost their way and spoke out turn, or against another, men the logical worker outa women roll, to guide them back onto the right level if the should travel to far in the unknown. WE reap what we sow, and this is the moral behind all our action, thoughts words and movements. Our live revolves around our words over time, so when we reap what we sow, sow if we pluck these words from the past present put into the future we be able to under further ahead then we first thought.

To start with nursery rhyme the COW JUMPED OVER THE MOON,, Every planet has a moon around them some have more, gods reasoning in this is to light the way. by sending our wisdom words over to next level, The cow jumped over the moon, little dog laugh to see such fun dish ran away with the spoon, moral behind this nursery rhyme, is we reap what we sow, jupiter has four moons, when we sent our wisdom words over the moon to next levels, to understand or improve further then it would come back again, There and back to see how far it is, moon carry the wise words over the seas far away, then as cloud formations move around as people travellers, then come back to start the prosess again For year mankind has been trying to work out find a way, to survive in human form on earth to eternity the way less travelled, has been found, in past time gods would take our sins from us, send them out into universe, keep the good energy force on us so we thought our sin had all gone and forgotten, but over centries, and time as generations grew part of the energy force where our sins keeped came back and have to be used to balance weather. By understanding the wisdom of our words he had found use for words, words and more words, as they double up and mulitply in cloud formation and is whats causing the extreme weather back to earth, horoscopes numeroledgy, technowledgy all have a purpose and use in this day age to send learn and rotate around world to other to improve and learn further of our passage in time for all human survival.

TWO MEANING TO EVER THING, MATERIAL POSSESSION ONE AND A SPIRITUAL ONE.

AND GROWING UP AS HUMAN FORM. The growing up part what we over look as important in our time, see how gods got it ready for us to understand, only when our minds can handle it by levels. where ever one may be let one wise word go free, when it come back Improve further or understand the level. See two meaning again. BY theories the growing up part our life span tall poppies, the top is our subconscious minds what we can't put into word, the middle when we stop, look, think, talk, with words verbally words, the bottom, is the part we reap tension stop think before we speak, apply patience with our mouth and action, this how the wise old owl became wise they created the nursery rhymes so children minds stayed down on level they could understand.

WE FOUND A way to stay alive in human form to eternity on earth and how it can be done in fairness to all mankind,man have been looking for the answer to this for centries but never could find the way god intended us to follow, we got so far and stopped learning put material possession first ahead of life, and survival, we grew up hearing that god will have peace on earth as in heaven, thy will be done, but he made us in his image to help him with his plan,was to stay alive in human form. we had the whole universe to conquer. REMEMBER, man in over years have tried to find the way, on how to stay alive in human form but couldn't. Until now we have found a way that will keep all humans alive until eternity as the gods promise, As said before we weren,t created to get old die, gods created humans to stay alive in human form on earth to help him with his plan. what better insentive, and guild lines to follow grow in body sole and mind.

WE ARE LIVING TO DIE, INSTEAD OF living to STAY ALIVE,

All inclined to live to die instead of living to stay alive in human form, ON EARTH. living for today and to hell with tomorrow only leads to early grave, gods created us to stay alive in human form until eternity on earth, the more we rotate our words understand wisdom of them the more we balance the weather and keep the elements from the universe at bay. If what bible states men lived to 200 odd years and women having babies at age over hundred, then this tells us something, why when most these day die arond 80 odd. so when we look at whole picture it boild s down to the fact. that we have stopped learning improving and understand why reason 4 our being running around and around others getting no where, so to look at whole picture, of one life span we had it all before, and elements from the universe suffocated earth by extreme weather dust and energy force we had no control over. with buried cities being found we have no options but to believe in this to could be true.

Be honest with ones selve, write down theories, wonders. first time one heard or understood part of the wisdom words tree it has to be done in writng by all so no one gets left behind this time. So much to get spread out in the energy force to build pillars and balance out the weather as we go.

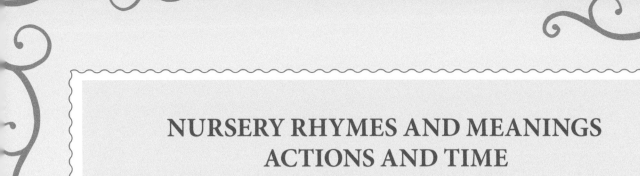

NURSERY RHYMES AND MEANINGS
ACTIONS AND TIME

CINDERRELLA AND GOLDEN SLIPPERS, A rolling stone gather no moss, tower of the four winds, turtle and the hare, old mother hubbard, mother goose, I'm a little tea pot, wise old owl, walk a crooked mile. These and plentry more all have adult meaning to them and play a major role in time. pick one one liked the best, when young or which one liked the best.

Adult meanings our action in our lives against others, we have learnt from, just nine of my favourites, like ten commandments, the ones we remeber are the one we most likely to act in in our life span,against other, based one theories, vision, thoughts wonders, actions, from birth to adult hood, The action they forgot was we had to live by these rules, not say them, and blaming other when our own mistakes surfaced. Back in times of yesteryear, The swear words.

Cinderella and golden slippers, this is one nursery ryhme that over centries we all went out and copied. the actions against others, how it originated was if one person wanted something or needed it the jealously of other would over shadow there thoughts and want same thing. Right down all generation, to thus far we have copied the same action against others. JEALOUSLY= WANTING TO BE FIRST, BETER THEN ANOTHER, there is no I want, or I SAID THAT, IN GODS VOCULABURY, once one become an adults, spiritually or verbally when one a child one carry on like that. Cinderella, morals behind this nursery rhymes is, as humans we all trieds to do this fit up same family tree path, when by branching out we could expaned and make more room for generation to come and spread out the energy force as the path to this was easiest way, but we eneded up with a tip at the top, with no where to go but down on our past mistakes,wich gets repeated over over again. As they call it history repeats its self in ever second generations this is the error we can prevent into the furthers of tomorrows. just goes to show how the answer are all in the bible. This how it can be done. Words like these short ones and number will put block out into the pillars to keep them strong in place, keep that spring in the gaps to balance the weather patterns.

JEALOUSLY= 131-14-5 (131)one can match these number up to any verse in bible and the verse match up to the words. One The scroll the bible talks about has exactly what I'm trying to explain in words written on it, tells us how it can be done, words from jealously= SLY, SEA . YES, YELL, USE.

TURTLE AND THE HARE, The hare raced ahead of the turtle for his own selfish agenda, The turtle took his time and got the path way through to perfection, OUR OLD TIME SAYING CAME FROM THIS ACTION, was cleaning their bodies not their minds, O(they left there muistakes on other or against other which block other view to see whats in front of them, the hare went to far out couldnt get back in again his mistakes blocked his was in.

The wise old owl sat in a tree(family tree)most familyies have a wise child, so can handle both sides family trees, other will follow iether mother father side to understand further. The less he spoke the more he heard, words old time saying, silence is golden, never speak until spoken to, the shoe didnt fit any one but the one it was meant for. So life like this one can,t go into another family tree life span which don't belong to ones by learning understand step by step we graudully move in the next levels. With confusion in this day age best to write it down wiat for right answer to what one wants to understand further,. it will come if one wonder about it. Like when I was a child. I'd wonder why some people were dark others whitc, how could it be, on off I'd think about it but when aI about forty the answer can to me now I do know the whole reason behind culture dark black brown white, ods got his finger in ever pie of wisdom cultures and words we speak and has a place in time when it all be needed to help with his plan.

Walk a crooked mile. One only needs to say one word out line and it will mutiply around others ten fold, THESE NURSERY RHYMES ORIGINATED FOR CHILDREN TO KEEP THEIR LITTLE MINDS DOWN ON LEVELS THEY CAN UNDERSTAND ABOUT LIFE, UNTIL OLD ENOUGH TO UNDERSTAND THE ADULTS MEANING TO THEM.

If ANY ONE OF US GO TO FAR IN ANYONE DIRECTION BEFORE OUR TIME WE BRING IN STUFF OUR MIND DON'T AND CAN'T UNDERSTAND AS WISDOM OF THE WORDS COULD POSSIBLE BELONG TO UNOTHER FAMILY TREE, TO WALK A CROOKED MILE, TO PUT ONE MISTAKES ON ANOTHER or to hide then underneath, these words written or spoken will at one time of our lives come back at us to understand wisdom of them.

I've picked two birds sparrow swallow both spelt simialar, look simialar, bounce around.

Instead living to die, live to live, a long life, in human form as we found a way. Go back to what one first knew and start again. Pick up pieces (mistakes) understand wisdom of the words of them. By our wisdom words don't try understand more then mind can handle at any given time, once corrected mistakes in children they back parent what they don't understand, then adults stop at age of 3oty and after that is wisdom word s years up down our own family tree more mistakes we correct the more we open up universe balance weather and make plenty room for all culture move around in, most what we do in life we turn to material possessions, but for got whats above our heads, the air we breath. The wisdom we forgot and the hole in top our heads we forgat that matches gods as he made us in his image

THIS just the tip ice berg floating around our lives energy force family trees and out into the universe.

All the action we do on earth has a spiritual meanings and images that form in the universe, what we do down below earth, is what comes in form wise words from above. To be understood and passed around to others to improve or understand. What goes around comes around, on level to understand. The top level wise words letters.

BIRDS OF A FEATHER STAY TOGETHER SPARROW = SWALLOW= TWO -RR TWO-LL., WALL. ARRROW. THE WALL WE BUILD AGAINST EACH OTHERS, THE ARROW CUPID RIGHT ETERNAL PARTNERS.

S,=P,A,R,R,O,W,= SEASONS, SEAS SOUND. = P, = PATTERNS PLACE PEOPLE, A=LL ahead, altar, air, R, RULERS, RAISE, RIGHT, = R ROWS RYHMES, REASONS, O= OFF OVER, ON, OUTER, W= WISDOM WISE WORDS, WONDER, WRITE, WORK,

THESE WORD ARE AND ACTION IN TIME, SEASONS SUMMER AUTUMN WINTER SPRING. NORTH EAST, SOUTH WEST, ALL COMBINED AND FITS IN THE FIRST LEVEL in time LIKE CLOCK FACE, THEN WIND MILL SHAPE, HEAD, SHOULDERS, BODY, LEGS ARMS FIRST EVER CREATED IN THE ENERGY FORCE OF UNIVERSE, We born with hole in head, which closes.as god was too, this hole was used to spout out at top unexplained wisdom and energy force that wasn't understood, he god sent it out top his head, like aspout. and bend over suck more in to be understood worked out in underneath then up through top his ho;e in his head, they became the spiritual god and those whom follow his path of survival. to become a spiritual god around our cultures and family trees, when one researches and understand vision one see. They realize that in this day age to fine hidden cities underground means we had it all before and the elements universe has suffocated earth, with out enough of populations and understand the true path we became stress ensed and got old and died, ever thing being created on earth has a meaning to our lives, and to improve further on to expaned the energy force above our heads.

When one looks at our words we speak and say ever day, seam to keep coming back in on us and we repeat them change them, but the end up surfacing on our children or other younger member family.

FOREWARD THINKING, THINKERS.

MAN -WOMEN BALANCE LEVELS,, GOD SAID, I'M THE BEGINNING THE END, FIRST THE LAST, FROM A-Z, 1-9 SO WHATS HE TELLING US I BELIEVE IS TO USE THE ALTHABET NUMBERS BREAK WORDS DOWN AND CHECK THEM WITH BIBLE VERSE, IT BASICALLY TELL ONE THE ANSWER TO LIFE MOST COMPLEX PROBLEM AND OUR REASON FOR BEING.

So take letters, S,S, W,T,M,R,SS=150-15-6 (150) PSALMS, PRAISE HIM TO HIS TEMPLE AND IN THE HEAVENS. HE MADE WITH MIGHTY POWER,PRAISE HIM FOR HIS MIGHTY WORKS, PRAISE HIS UNEQUALLED GREATNESS, (15) ANYONE WHOM LIVED A BLAMELESS LIFE AND IS TRULY SINCERE, ANY ONE WHO REFUSE TO SLANDER, ANOTHER DOES NOT LISTEN TO GOSSIP NEVER HARMS HIS NIEGHBOR SPEAKS OUT AGAINST SIN SUCH A MAN SHALL STALL FIRM FOREVER

EVER WORD WE SAY SWEAR WORDS NASTYNESS CAN ALL BE DONE IN THIS WAY, IT SPERADS OUT A WHOLE KNEW MEANING TO OUR LIFE SPAN HAS THE INTERESTS OF OTHER TO IMPROVE FURTHER.

TAKE THE WORD WALLS, 48-12- 3 (48) psalms, rising north city high above the plans, all to see joy to all earth, the residence of great gods. (12)go inspect the cities walk around inspect many towers of wisdom words note her wisdom words in many places so you can teach it to your children, (3)god himself is the defender, all earth and heaven and in between. The words are the walls as we stopped learning and improving on the family tree of our wise words and wonders.

Now what this verse is tring to explain and say is,inspect the wisdom words that surround the wall of ever family member has got thus far, this wall in our time. Is when we go back to what we first knew and start again, pick up our mistakes correct them then understand the wisdom of our mistake, we make the mistake over time in firsts place, as our minds all determine them differently, our subconsious minds know the truth on how to proceed but our conscious mind determine it differently, that why we get branches on our family trees as we all branch out different ways,then back again to main trunk which while young is our parents, (old time saying fits there, is there and back see how far it is.)

This verse, very interesting its what happening in our days now. There is 7 gods surrounding our family tree spiritual each ones got a eye on how we proceed and help us to take next step. These words in bible are true to form spiritual god the god above all other gods. heavenly god, almighty god, lord god, god, Jesus, two women gods got to this level understanding they to are protecting us in our pathway of steps.

Now wake up strengthen what little remains, for even that whats left is at the point of death, your deeds are far from right, in sight gods, go back to what you first heard. And believe at first hold to it firmly. And turn to me again, this message is sent to you by one whom is holy and true and has the key to open whaT =NO ONE CAN SHUT AND SHUT ANY DOOR NO ONE CAN OPEN, = This means that what ive said before in this book to exspanned it further in words of understanding is to go baCK TO YOUR BIRTH PICK UP PIECES AND CORRECT PAST MISTAKES THEN UNDERSTAND THE WISDOM OF WORDS, iN LIFE THE TRUTH WILL ALWAYS SURFACE, SO TO HIDE OUR MISTAKES AGAINST OTHER BEHIND UNDERNEATH OR TRY OVER THE TOP, ITS ALL BE TRIED IN PAST TIMES, NEVER YET SEEN IT WORK FACE TO FACE WITH GODS THUS FAR. Every thing we think say and do comes back at us from day we born once reach 50plus, We grow we make mistakes, then compounded around our waist like a belt it clings, until we understand the wisdom of our words, we get held back till death onset. this is when gods say to one . now wake up strenghten what little remains for even that whats left is at point death, this door is now opening for those whom want to help other understand,remember, gods made us in their image to help him with his plans to conquer the whole unibverse, REMEMBER, THIS IS ONE WAY IT CAN BE DONE IN FAIRNESS TO ALL MANKIND

The words flow as the speedest writer, on how it can be done

LIFE MOST COMPLEX PROBLEMS

THE REAL REASON 4 OUR BEING

LIVE AND LET LIVE DON,T LIVE TO DIE

LIVE TO STAY ALIVE TO ETERNITY

My inspirational wisdom words passage in time

The waywards winds based on, theories, vision thoughts wonder, wise, old saying songs and nursery rhymes.and verse from bible all parts of the words laid on our person, from birth to adulthood, research, and science, in this life gods sent me to the pits hell to find the answer the devil hid there, I rose back up through time we help others wise ones, with and how we can all stay alive in human form untill eternity as promised by the gods, peace on earth as in heaven, we were shut out heaven gate closed till we learnt right way. when one puts ones life action faults, wonder, together one finds out more ever day, about the reason for our being. IT ALL ADDS UP TOGETHER FROM DAY WE BORN OUR BORN DAY, TILL TIME WE DIE THE MORE WE LEARN UNDERSTAND THE MORE WE STAY ALVE IN HUMAN FORM, we open up the heavens energy force and balance out the weather patterns as we go. there so much more to our lives them meets the eye have we had it all before, made a mistake and broke the universe apart thus far we had gone, does our subconious mind know the true but our conscious mind determines our words action and thoughts differently. and is the branching out in different direction in our family trees important then back again to the center, the center of partents and imediate family

THE WORLD AN OYSTER, ALL WE GOT TO DO IS PLUCK IT, ON RIGHT LEVEL UNDERSTANDING, wisdom words, our own family tree first. MOST THESE OLD TIME SAYING IN THIS BOOK IS ONE., myself have an interest in these words wisdom always keeped me wondering what they meant. or mean, over time I saw two side to them a material possession and a spiritual one. Like the one about it was never a race who got their first it was a race we all get it right before its to late. and elements universe suffocated earth by weather patterns. Nursery rhyme The turtle and the hare.

The other one of interests, as was said in my growing up days of wonder. Always watch the quite ones?,

Now this one I often wonder about, "what did it mean" I looked inside my self to see if i was like that was I sneaky child is that what these wise words meant. so when I corrected that part my nature, I then realized how these words,old saying had a deeping improtant meaning. the wisdom of these words were the important part, to understand, like the wise old owl whom sat in the family trees the more they spoke the more he heards, he listened and learnt, So when we flock togethers in groups, we find our words get entangled into others conversations and we start a sentence then can,t finish what we were thinking about, as part of what we were think got block inothers words, so we all misunderstand what each others saying our mind determine their conversations differently.

Did It mean being quite mean one was sly, sneaky, and selfish, or did it mean by watching the quite one, ones would learn a lot about life passage in time, Like the wise old, owl who sat in trees(family tree) more he listened the more he heard, Silence was golden, By not speaking until spoken too .verbally, over time we found people were answering out line, as there mistakes against other were coming back at them and a converstaion between two people got a lot interference, of voices, when one meets right eternal partners and each go out into public arena, there relationship built on trust they go seperate ways during day, come back at nights put the wise words, actions, together teach children them whats not understood goes back out above adults heads,this action is survival mode in time,

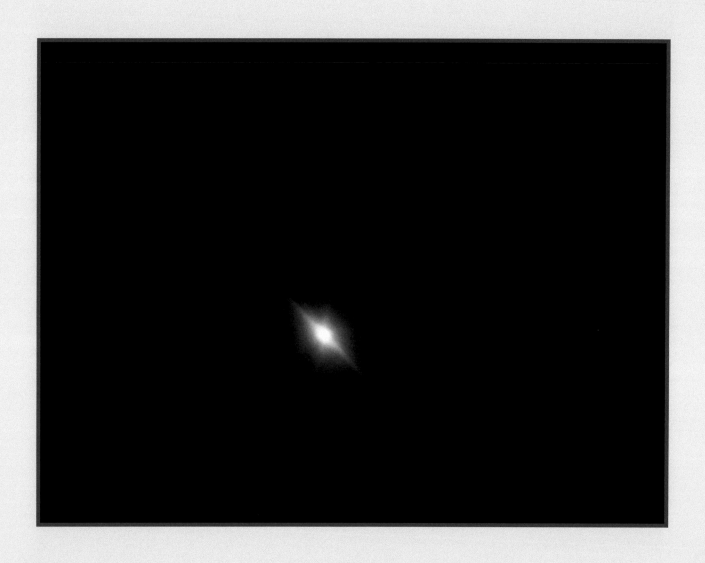

I choose sparrow, swallow as they birds I saw lot of while growing up. the other bird was a sky lark, it would hoover over the ground looking to nest.

The SKY LARK, this verse in psalms tells exctly how the swear word become about, we being told not to swear, blame or judge others but this verse tells us how the swear word become about and also tell us what part in time they can be used, to balance weather how. These verse tells another way of understand gods true path to survival. some people automatically understand other read or need it said to them verbally, but it all begins at our birth, teenage years and then adult hood, this is when we get complications, we forgot what we left behind on others so or bodies grow weak and our spirits deminish, we give up as no one else has learnt with us to advance furture into the umknown, of history and survival made.

SKYLARK=95=14-5 (95) TO 96- VERSES

OH COME LET US SING TO THE LORD. songs over time helps ease the tension energy force, or helps us not to speak out turn.

Give a joyous shout, in land of the rock of our salvations, (1for the lords the great god above all gods He controls formations of the depts of earth and mightest mountains, are all his. he made the seas, formed the land, they to are his, for he is our god, . we are his sheep dont harden your heart as he did in past times wilderness, for they doublted lord, who seen so many gods miricle before my patience have run thin, and severly tried, by thier complaints, for forty years I watched in digust, The lord god says They were a nation who thoughts and hearts were far away they refused to except, my laws there for mighty wrath I swore, that would never enter, the promised land the place of rest I planned for them. The swear words, originated at this time in history and how it became about, but the greatness of god found away to use gods wrath over this to be used later in time to balamce our weather prevent the extreme storm, his wrath anger and swear words split the energy force, up to give space in between the planets,, The force of these swear words scattered throught out time, and down generation over time,, the wall, the rock, and the levels we all on

THE SPARROW AND THE SWALLOW, TWO L,L, TWO R,R. L,ONG L,IVES R,ULERS, R,AISED, TWO, W, WORDS, WISE, tunnel vision is another view we can hear say and understand wisdom path, tunnel vision is the middle part our time. we only see as far as our mistakes against others, when this happened people tried to go over the top underneath gods chair, but the middle give us a chance to go face to face with gods, so he they can open next level or door, to one path, in time

THIS CHAPTER BOUT HOW TO BREAK DOWN WORDS IN VERSE OF THE BIBLE TO GET A ANSWER TO LIFE MOST COMPLEX PROBLEMS.

It so sad to hear people say they live for day and to hell with tomorrow, and are living to die, as in past years we didn't know any better once we got old we prepared ourselves to die, but the reason being is we lost our way, became so ingrossed into a one way path of material possession we forgot to explore the outer skirts of heaven gate, our passage in time for all human survival, centreis ago people lived for over two hundred years and women had babies over hundred, so this two explains that we must had it all before made a mistake and lost our way, was this wisdom rotated around to other planets was the light passage through to planets like mars venus mercury up to earth, did earth the only planet survived with weather around, were we rejenrated agiain has been seen by vision a white passage through to these planets of past forefather mother wise wisdom words.

This is where the bible say write ones vision down as one day they will be need and once something written down the images vision words one mind never forgets.

WE ALL HAVE VISION THROUGH TIME BUT WE ONLY SEE AS FAR AS THE ONE WE MADE OR LAID A MISTAKES ON, THE BIBLE HAVE ALL THE ANSWER BUT ITS A MATTER OF WHAT ART IN TIME WE AS INDIVIGUALS WANT TO LEARN UNDERSTAND MORE ABOUT ITS ALL CONNECTED, EARTH LAND SEA AIR, WORDS WISDOM AND OUR MOVEMENTS AND ACTIONS, thoughts wonders, ideas vision.

The out courts are the energy force above our heads in cloud formations with words and tension and thought that keeps us spinning around the universe, the main words ive picked, is LIGHTNING, BULLING, WALL,FIRE SMOKE,, LIGHTNING 100-10-1) NUMEROLEDGY,REVERLATIONS VERSES, (10) LIGHTNING,= Then I saw another mighty angel, coming down from heaven surrounded by a cloud, with a rainbow over his head, his face shone like the sunand his feet flashed with fire, he held open in his right hand a scrollhe set his right foot on the seas his left foot on earth, and gave a great shout, it was like the roar of a lion and the seven thunder crashed thier reply.(13) justice goes before him to make a path way for his steps.

Also this was given to women as thier gift in life, to help guide men on right path on levels, keep them into their own path in time, day time go different direction night time come home and sort out the wisdom words what wasnt understood went up to gods and what was understood was brought in to the children, in nursery rhymes songs to keep mind down to a level they could understand.but most in our day are still in primitive days of thinking to understand exaxtly what this role intails, they are able to guide man back on track with out saying words verbally, some where, along the way they to have lost there way. I believe we had it all before made a mistake broke the engry force apart above our head and had to start from scratch again, on earth today women have the gift to be foreward thinkers.relationship built on trust one didnt venture into a private affair, or gave advise where it wasnt asked for, all these mistakes we still living and doing against others, with out touching whats not thier before their time. or were, man are the logical worker outers, that work things out in their mind then to women then women to children its all wise words and wisdom of our time.

I WAS ABOUT TO WRITE IT DOWN WHEN A VOICE. from heaven said "dont do that these words are not to be revealed.then the seventh angel blows his trumpet revealed the plan mysteruos through the ages ever since it was annouced, the swear words we use today, but once broken down into numeroledgy and verse its all wisdom words and has a place in time when it be used to help balance the weather patterns out one swear words god spoke these words in anger as people werent learning, the right path, so to correct his angry words he said if one could find the hidden words wisdom devil hide in hell then he would open any door no one can shut to his people to find their way back to heaven.

word= f,u,c,k,== stretched words= future under center kingdom, a path in time,

word = h,e,l,l. == heaven eternal long life, the whole universe to conquer remember,

word = e,v,i,l, == enternal vision inner lives. tunnel vision, broad vision, long sighted,

word = d,e,v,i,l===distance eternal visions in life. means long sighted.

Foreward thinkers, or thinking. This is the role that gods gave to women, to help balance our lives on levels, Walls are the reason our words block our way verbally and spiritually two walls a brick wall spiritual wall

WALLS-(48-12-3(48)Rising north city high above in plain view all to see joy all the earth residence great gods. (12) go inspect the city walls walk among many toweer of wisdom words note her words are many pieccs so you can teach them to your children .same understanding as honor thy father and mother, learn from their mistake correct them in children. (I am my father daughter nomatter ho my father is. 0 (3) GOD HIMSELF IS THE DEFENDER, OF ALL EARTH and heaven and in between. The black wall is the wall to keep us in safety from elements of universe.

To match up with verse. psalms The key to this words actions we have to live by them. In ever thing we think say do, so the values we taught as children prevent us from straying out side the family tree before our time, by living by these values our path opens up tenfold.

thinking=92-11-2(92) its good to say thank-you to the lord the god above all gods, (its the spiritual god)(10) I have heard the doom of my enemies, announced and seen them distroyed but the godly shall flourish like palm trees, (or family trees) and grow tall like the cedar (2)ever nmorning tell him thank you ever evening rejoice in his faithfullness.

foreward= 85-13-4(85) lord you have planned out Amazing blessing to this land and fore givven sins at your people covered over everone . (13) justice goes before him to make a path way for his steps, (4) now bring us back to loving you oh lord so that your anger will never need to rise against us again. (this anger they say is the block to prevent one from going to far in wrong direction, no gods anger its the wall to prevent wrong stuff from universe from covering over.

11-2-(11) REVERLATIONS=

(11)Now I was given a measuring stick and told to go measure the temple of gods, encluding inner court where the alter stands count the number of worshipers,but do not measure the outer court, I was told as they have been turned over to the nations . (so what this verse is saying the nations working acting out the motions of the tension energy force around their bodies, send it up to heavens gods to work out the wisdom way of them then send it back down to be the globe of life go between the gods down to courts the down to the people the main trunk of the trees we we have created in to a family tree of levels, understand.

(2) I write to inform you of those who walk among the churches and holds the leaders in his right hand.

Reverlations- foreward 13-4- and now in my vision I saw a strange creature rising up out of the seas 7 heads ten horns ten crowns upon his head, (very first part of time before humans formed,(4) then I looked and saw a door standing open in heavens and sound of the voice i,d heard before thats sound like a mighty trumpet blast spoke me and said command I will show you what must happen in future, instantly I was in heaven in spirit, 'oh the glory."

Now over time we all gets parts bible coming in on us in words and past actions for our minds to understand in this day age our time, what was seen in heaven was shown how for us to proceed into future through d god wisdom words path and use our words past present to balance the clouds formations, as we go .bible states to use the number althabet, and match them to the verse in bible, by doing this we keep alive our true passage, parts bible verse are all mixed up from differet part time we lived in, so its very much like a jig -saw puzzle as generation go on we sort the verse out into right chaper of our words reason theories, and vision, the reason behide all this is to open up heavens and peace on earth as in heaven, we won,t get peace until the works is done remember we have the whole universe to conquer.

FOREWARD THINKERS AND FOREWARD THINKING,

WORDS, this phrase verse once words Started up we learnt to speak, ONCE WE SPOKE WE USED WORDS AGAINST OTHER FOR DIFFERENT REASON

WORDS 19-10-1)(19) (16) what word have become over life and have Confused, distroyed and caused rows in families, oh god yopur land has being conquered by heathens nation your temple is defiled, in heap ruins, (means words have got out control against others, past times, as they maltiply in to different form over time. they become more and more away from the true path to follow, the path in time has become less travelled and we lossing our way to the survival human life.

(7) For they have distroyed our peoples invading every home (family tree) oh do not hold us guilty for our former sins let your tender hearts mercies meet our needs.

7 plagues on earth, what are they, wind rain, sunshine, north, east, south, west, four corner of earth.

Verse from Reverlation.

NORTH= 75-12-3(75) THE GREAT PAGNAINT APPEARED IN HEAVEN PORTRAYING THINGS TO COME, SAW A WOMEN CLOTHERED WITH THE SUN, MOON BENEATH HER FEET CROWN TWELVE STARS UPON HER HEAD

(12) This message is sent to you by one who has the 7 fold spirit of gods, and 7 stars,, the seven fold spirits is the seven gods, surround earth our lives and send messages to us to follow,

East=45)(9) then the 5th angel blew his trumpet and I saw one who had fallen to earth from heaven, and to him was given the key to the bottomless pit, belief over time hs it that the devil took all gods wise ways done and hide them in the pitts of hell, and people got confused of the right wrong of things words and actions, so god sent his wisest women down pits hell to retrieve his vision wise words and bring up top to save human life and earth.

South 83-11-(83)(11) now I was given measuring stick and told to go out measure the temple and inner court where alter stands and count number of worshipers, (2) but not measure out courts, for its being turned over to the nations. this action over time explains how they measured the distance between earth and energy force that surround our action and weather words forcasts.

West=67-13-4 (13) there as I looked I saw a strange creatures rising up from the seas, it had 7 heads and 10 horns and 10 crowns upon the horns (this part in time probable before humans were born is very interesting and has insight into how god created us in first place.

(13) Then as I look I saw a door open in heaven and same vioce I'd heard before that sounded like a mighty trumpet, blast, spoke to me and said come, here and ill show you whats happens in futures to come and instantly, I was in heaven in spirit and saw oh the glory of it a throne and some one sitting on it in great bust of light, the first bet in time was between gods and the devil if god created human being they'll end up distroying each other. The devils well laid plans to hide gods wisdom path down pits hell was, misguided when god sent his wisest angel down to retrieves his wisdom, as the angel found a way to use the devil words distruction and blinding people to the truth of survival, in human form til eternity on earth, As the devil known to have said that if god create human they end up distroying themselves and each others. The devil would have won but for his angel of mercy he sent below, to pick up pieces, on how to progress into the futhers for all mankind and worked out a way humans can stay alive in human form till eternity, but devil lossing big time as we way ahead devil and his evil nasty way of life will be used to balance out the weather patterns, and gods use these extreme words as his pillars to ae strong in place .

Ever word will have its uses, once discarded form our levels eduction or repeating same old same old over over agin against each other, doubled up words be sent out to put weather around other planets, if we get it right on earth first rest planets be easy.

I am the first the last the beginning the end from a-z from 1=9 (it say use alphabet a number in further progress understanding).

The one word causes most problems in life, from childhood and through out adulthood.

Word Jealously, WORDS INSIDE, SEA, SLY, WALLS yells use yes

Jealously=(131-14-5(131) I am not proud haughty, I don't, think myself better then others, I don't pretend to know it all I am quite now before the lord. just as a child, who has been weened from the breats . yes my begging has stilled you all to should quitely trust the lord now and always.

Our words do match the verse in bible and give greater meanings to our path passage to survivel as, as we go we have to balance out clouds weather patte

To open any door no one can shut, shut any door no one can open, to get to the gods one has to go by Jesus first(how to do this to take footstep understanding one has to look inside them selve correct own mistake of others, an understand own nature habits wrongs.

Cleaning ones body not their minds, RACING AHEAD LEAVING MISTAKES BEHIND, LIKE A RING A RING A ROSY, ROUND AND ROUND THE MOULDERY BUSH, GETTING NO WHERE IN TIME, NURSERY RHYMES PLAYED A BIG PART IN OUR DEVELOPEMENT, IN MIND BODY AND SOLE, BUT THE KEY TO IT ALL WE HAD TO LIVE BY THEM STEP BY STEP

Saying of timeS, cleaning one body and not their minds, for ones self first only leads to a passage of no return as other infront or behind waiting in line the right way for next level in tiem or own family trees or wisdom words, as people identify with bible words and wisdom . songs oldtime saying and vision, bible, wise words.

THE GODS NUMBER. (8) GODS KNOW US WELL WE ARNT STRONG BUT WE TRIED TO OBEY AND HAVE NOT DENIED MY NAME THEREFORE IVE OPENED A DOOR TO YOU THOU NO ONE CAN SHUT.

Beside the ten command ment being the short cut to survive on eather in human form the short cut to understand the true meanings of words of the bible. The answer are all in the bible each and ever one of us wonder about, Back in days of gods he got to the stage of impatience with the moaning whinning of his followers, so in anger he shouted out to the with swear words, the bible states these word never to be spoken or taught. But in verse 95, in psalms, it says about this. With the wondering why people blamed god for being angry with them Id think gods not angry with them he and because they weren't listening to his path way on, and so he shut the door on them, with angry word until they learnt the right way.

This is the repeats of history down generation, same mistakes against each other over and over again as we still can't grasp what path god intended us to follow. But know we have found a way. This leads me to another vision I HAD about whats ahead in the future, once we get it right. what my thought patterns saw by vision, and believes through wonder is is there really another planet further out what we call heaven, and us that generate on earth are the prduct form the rubbish gets pushed out heaven wise word not understood by heavens way, is earth or the planets out side earth jupiter, the rubbish dump for all misunderstood wisdom from heaven, keep open mind about this have we all had it before and as some us tried to do it our own way, god sent us down in the pits to find way back up to his way of thinking and rotating wisdom words, I aw something by vision that my mind couldnt comprehend at the time.

The bible states go back to what one first knew, and turn to me again .back to birth pick up our pieces we left behind and start all over this time we should learn from our mistakes on all levels, we lost our way as the devil words confused us, and made god angry, so he shut the door on us until we learnt the right way,when a person repeats ones self or gets angry that means there a mistakes coming in on them they left on anothers.

GODS MESSAGE THIS WISDOM WORDS WAY CAN BE DONE IN FAIRNESS TO ALL MANKIND AND CULTURE, THE REASON BEING TO BALANCE OUT THE WEATHER PATTERNS AS WE GO. LIFE BEGAN AND ENDS WITH GODS WISEST PEOPLE AND THOSE WHOM LIVE TO STAY ALIVE AND SACRIFICE THIER LIVE UPON GODS ALTAR THEY THEN BECOME WISE, This book unviels some of the future activities soon to accur in life Jesus Christ, gods permitted him to reveal these things to his people. seen in vision and then the angel who was sent from heaven, to explain vision meanings, told to write it all down the words of gods and jesus of ever thing he heard and saw, by vision, for time is near when these things will come true, so one see how the bible words verse, does play a big part in our everday lives to survive, and to prevent history from repeating its self, over and over again. the days have come when it has to be done in writing to get the right levels of understanding and put more pillars out there to brace and hold back extreme weather patterns.

OPEN THE DOOR ========= your mind======WITH OUR WORDS==========
To life most complex problems, THE REAL REASON 4OUR BEING

help unravel life most enormous jig saw puzzle of time.

when you come into my family trees The doors open, but when one leaves don,t stand in doorway as ones blocking the wisdom words flowing through Where ever one may be let your wise words go free when they come back improve on

them what comes around goes around

Don,t stand behind me I may not lead, Don,t stand in front of me i may not follow Just stand beside me and we work it out together wisdom words way in fairness to all mankind

DONT let the devl in or he always want to drive, Do we know exaclty what kind mistakes we are doing aginst other.

First we start as a child brother sister mother father, what do we learn about getting our own way, playing one parent against The other and with brother sister to, this well good when young, but do we realize that in teens and adult hood we use same tacktic to getwhat we want in material possessions,

but we forget the barrier we put up between oursevles and god in understand how to work the element in the universe.

so when bible verse state to go back to the start, hold close what you learn in the beginning then come back to me again,start agiain

UNDER (3) verse revelation, say now wake up strengthen what little that remains, for evens what left as a part in sight of god, (means god can still get through to some of the people on earth the right passage in time. Turn to me again, unless you do i will come down on you sunddenly. as its not god doing it we doing it to our selves as we taken a wrong turning in his passage of life, an human survival.

Turn back to me-he says- so go back to your childhood start again this time one has life experiences with them, start at birth, dont look for your mistake they find you when the times right for it to be corrected on levels, ahead. AS one children grow one see them act out ones mstakes or they may ask about them. this when adutls understand the wisdom of them, once they have corrected them to thier children, honor thy father mother learn from there mistakes correct them in your children is true path to follow. no other path will lead one to the heavens above, when one return to own childhood, and come back up with the experience form past mistake they pickup the pieces that left behind understand the wisdom words way, god send his messages to indiviguals on levels their mind understand at any given time. the right message at the right time only meant for the one he sends them to not another to speak out on, as the confused and dismayed, in our lives today most the true messages send from god, the minds determine them all differently, this over time is why the family tree got created . as ideas how and what the meassage meant or means branched out in a different track from others,, this in gods eye is good as it was easier to suck in energy force from universe to open up heaven and earths moving passage, through time and elements of theuniverse. .,

PITS of hell, we rise up and down our life span, over our growing up, when we t the top we should take care as what we laid on other on way down will smack us in the face, patience is and always be the key,

when we travellers through other time and life span, as if we touch whats not our before our time, we bring stuff in on us our minds not ready to understand yet, and this inturn causes anger tension voilance and sometimes death to our selves loved ones and friends.

when we go down to pits hell as the say, then we come back up right way, through our own family trees wisdom words, live by them, and improve further one what we understand, the more us older one improve and understand in wisdom terms the more the next generation improve further again, this is the nursery rhyme of the adult meaning, hickory dickory dock, the mouse ran up the clock, when it got to top the clock struck one the mouse ran down again, sprinkling out the wisdom words to improve further, acros to one two three,, inhuman life one

THE END PART BOOK,

THE GODS NUMBER. (8).I GODS KNOW US WELL WE ARNT STRONG BUT WE TRIED TO OBEY AND HAVE NOT DENIED MY NAME THEREFORE IVE OPENED A DOOR TO YOU THOU NO ONE CAN SHUT, GODS MESSAGE THIS WISDOM WORDS WAY CAN BE DONE IN FAIRNESS TO ALL MANKIND AND CULTURE, THE REASON BEING TO BALANCE OUT THE WEATHER PATTERNS AS WE GO. LIFE BEGAN AND ENDS WITH GODS WISEST PEOPLE AND THOSE WHOM LIVE TO STAY ALIVE AND SACRIFICE THIER LIVE UPON GODS ALTAR THEY THEN BECOME WISE.

THE GODS NUMBER. (8).I GODS KNOW US WELL WE ARNT STRONG BUT WE TRIED TO OBEY AND HAVE NOT DENIED MY NAME THEREFORE iVE OPENED A DOOR TO YOU THOU NO ONE CAN SHUT, GODS MESSAGE THIS WISDOM WORDS WAY CAN BE DONE IN FAIRNESS TO ALL MANKIND AND CULTURE, THE REASON BEING TO BALANCE OUT THE WEATHER PATTERNS AS WE GO. LIFE BEGAN AND ENDS WITH GODS WISEST PEOPLE AND THOSE WHOM LIVE TO STAY ALIVE AND SACRIFICE THIER LIVE UPON GODS ALTAR THEY THEN BECOME WISE, this book unviels some of the future activities soon to accur in life Jesus Christ, gods permitted him to reveal these things to his people. seen in vision and then the angel who was sent from heaven, to explain vision meanings, told to write it all down the words of gods and jesus of ever thing he heard and saw, by vision, for time is near when these things will come true, so one see how the bible words verse, does play a big part in our everday lives to survive, and to prevent history from repeating its self, over and over again. the days have come when it has to be done in writing to get the right levels of understanding and put more pillars out there to brace and hold back extreme weather patterns.

Printed in the United States
By Bookmasters